BIOGRAPHY FROM
ANCIENT CIVILIZATIONS
LEGENDS, FOLKLORE, AND STORIES OF ANCIENT WORLDS

The Life and Times of

GENGHIS KHAN

Mitchell Lane
PUBLISHERS

P.O. Box 196
Hockessin, Delaware 19707

BIOGRAPHY FROM
ANCIENT CIVILIZATIONS
LEGENDS, FOLKLORE, AND STORIES OF ANCIENT WORLDS

Titles
in the Series

The Life and Times of:

BIOGRAPHY FROM
ANCIENT CIVILIZATIONS
LEGENDS, FOLKLORE, AND STORIES OF ANCIENT WORLDS

The Life and Times of

GENGHIS KHAN

Jim Whiting

Copyright © 2006 by Mitchell Lane Publishers, Inc. All rights reserved. No part of this book may be reproduced without written permission from the publisher. Printed and bound in the United States of America.

Printing   1   2   3   4   5   6   7   8
Library of Congress Cataloging-in-Publication Data

Whiting, Jim, 1943-
    The life and times of Genghis Khan / by Jim Whiting.
       p. cm. — (Biography from ancient civilizations)
    Includes bibliographical references and index.
    ISBN 1-58415-348-2 (lib. bdg.)
    1. Genghis Khan, 1162–1227. 2. Mongols—Kings and rulers—Biography. I. Title.
II. Series.
DS22.W45 2005
950'.21'092—dc22
                                            2004030258

ABOUT THE AUTHOR: Jim Whiting has been a journalist, writer, editor, and photographer for more than 20 years. In addition to a lengthy stint as publisher of *Northwest Runner* magazine, Mr. Whiting has contributed articles to the *Seattle Times*, *Conde Nast Traveler*, *Newsday*, and *Saturday Evening Post*. He has written numerous books for Mitchell Lane in a variety of series. He has also edited more than 100 Mitchell Lane titles. A great lover of classical music and ancient history, he has written many books for young adults, including *The Life and Times of Irving Berlin* and *The Life and Times of Julius Caesar* (Mitchell Lane). He lives in Washington state with his wife and two teenage sons.

PHOTO CREDITS: Cover, pp. 1, 3—Mansell/Time Life Pictures/Getty Images; p. 6—Superstock; pp. 12, 34—China Plate; pp. 20, 27—AsiaPacific; p. 23—Corbis; pp. 25, 30—Jamie Kondrchek; p. 36—Hulton Archive/Getty Images; p. 40—Giardini Botanici; p. 41—SBCEO.

PUBLISHER'S NOTE: This story is based on the author's extensive research, which he believes to be accurate. Documentation of such research is contained on page 47.

The internet sites referenced herein were active as of the publication date. Due to the fleeting nature of some web sites, we cannot guarantee they will all be active when you are reading this book.

BIOGRAPHY FROM ANCIENT CIVILIZATIONS

LEGENDS, FOLKLORE, AND STORIES OF ANCIENT WORLDS

The Life and Times of

GENGHIS KHAN

*For Your Information

Alexander the Great was one of history's greatest military commanders. When his father died in 336 B.C., Alexander became the king of Macedon, a region in modern-day Greece. In the next thirteen years, he conquered nearly 2,000,000 square miles of territory. He died at the age of 33, most likely of a fever.

CHAPTER
ONE

A MIGHTY EMPIRE

One of the most famous conquerors in history is Alexander the Great. He is among a handful of leaders who have been honored with the title "the Great" after their names. Born in 356 B.C. in Macedon, a region in northern Greece, Alexander became king at the age of twenty. Within the span of just over a decade, he and his army seized control of more than two million square miles of territory. His empire stretched from Greece and Egypt in the west to India in the east. Yet this sprawling empire couldn't survive its founder's death at the age of thirty-three. Alexander's generals soon began quarreling. Within a few years, the empire split up.

About fifteen centuries later, another conqueror emerged from the steppes and mountains of central Asia. This was Genghis Khan. Unlike Alexander, Genghis Khan's empire continued to expand after his death. Eventually it encompassed about 12 million square miles. It stretched nearly a quarter of the way around the globe—from China's coast to Hungary, from Russia in the north to the Persian Gulf in the south. Its vast size could easily have swallowed Alexander's empire. It could also have held the entire Roman Empire at its greatest extent, with room left over to add present-day Canada and the United States.

This mighty empire was established by a man, whose father was murdered. He was one of seven children of a suddenly widowed mother who was abandoned by her husband's kinsmen. For several years the boy and his family lived a desperate life in one of the planet's harshest climates, the Asian steppes, eating mice and scrounging for berries during winters when the temperature dropped well below freezing.

On a personal level, he showed few signs of future greatness. "As a child, he feared dogs and he cried easily," writes Jack Weatherford, a professor of anthropology whose studies have focused on Genghis Khan. "His younger brother was stronger than he was and a better archer and wrestler; his half brother bossed him around and picked on him."[1]

Somehow the boy managed to overcome these limitations and survive this precarious existence. In the decades to come, he did much more than just survive.

What is especially astonishing is that Genghis Khan and his successors amassed their empire with one of the smaller conquering armies in history. Researchers estimate that the size of the Mongol army was only between 100,000 and 130,000 men. Nearly all of them could have fit into the spectator seating in the Rose Bowl in Pasadena, California, with the rest standing on the football field. Very rarely did they all fight as one large group, and they were hundreds—and often thousands—of miles from home.

Leading this army, Genghis Khan acquired a gruesome reputation. He is alleged to have perpetrated some of the worst massacres in world history. When he captured the city of Bukhara in central Asia in 1219, his men killed all 30,000 defenders and drove the rest of the city's inhabitants in front of them as human shields in their next battle. Four years earlier, his troops had almost completely destroyed Zhongdu (modern Beijing). Later, travelers to the site found little besides human bones and skeletons of horses. According to contemporary chroniclers, millions of people perished at Genghis

Khan's direct command. However, many historians believe that these numbers are exaggerated. Genghis Khan understood psychological warfare. He knew that inflated estimates of casualties could strike fear in the hearts of his opponents. That could cause them to surrender or flee without a fight.

Whether their reputation for savagery is accurate or inflated, the Mongol armies hardly ever resorted to torturing their victims during their campaigns. And in another way, they "fought fair." Many of their attacks were against walled cities. They gave their intended victims two options. If the city surrendered without a fight, the inhabitants would be spared. If it chose to resist, the Mongols would attack and kill without mercy.

What is less well known is the flip side to this fearsome reputation. Once Genghis Khan's conquests were completed, most people lived in peace. He devised a code of laws that encouraged a high standard of morality. And his influence extended even beyond the empire's borders. While trade routes such as the Silk Road had been in existence before the rise of Genghis Khan, they were often dangerous. Genghis Khan and his successors instituted what historians call the *Pax Mongolica* (Mongolian Peace).

As historian Urgunge Onon notes, "The Mongols opened a transcontinental road between East and West along which, for the first time in one thousand years, humans and cultural objects and influences could once again be safely exchanged."[2] Technologies such as gunpowder, movable type, and printing made the long trek from east to west. So did new types of food, clothing, art, literature, and music. Some historians believe that these influences contributed to the Renaissance, the rebirth of learning that blossomed in Europe in the mid-fifteenth century.

Long before the invention of the telegraph and telephone in the nineteenth century, Genghis Khan realized that swift, reliable communications gave armies a big advantage over potential enemies. They also made it possible to govern his vast empire. He established a system that in its basic concept was similar to the Pony Express. In reality, it was much more complex and lasted far longer than its American counterpart, which folded after less than two years of operations. A system of relay stations spaced about 25 miles apart allowed riders on horseback to cover distances of up to 100 miles a day. In emergencies, they rode up to 250 miles. It was hard on the messengers. They forced themselves to stay on their horses for hour after hour, frequently fastening themselves to their saddles so that they wouldn't tumble off if they fell asleep.

As the centuries went by and the vast empire he founded—and its memories—began to fade, so did the reputation of Genghis Khan. Perhaps the low point came during the nineteenth century when Western scientists classified some non-European ethnic groups as "mongoloid." According to this classification, such people were not only very primitive but also suffered from genetic faults such as mental retardation.

The rise of Western imperialism was probably one primary reason for this disrespect. As countries such as France, Great Britain, and Russia began to dominate the globe, they felt that it was necessary to downplay the previous accomplishments of the people they were ruling. These countries believed that they were giving the benefits of "civilization" to the people who had fallen under their control. Their "civilized" behavior, much of which descended from Alexander the Great, was in contrast to the lifestyle of "barbarians" such as Genghis Khan.

In recent years, Genghis Khan's reputation has begun to increase again, especially among Asians. A book about him entitled *The No. 1 Man of the Last 1,000 Years* was published in China in 2003. He had achieved a similar standing a few years earlier when the *Washington Post*—one of the largest and most prestigious newspapers in the United States—asked many historians to name the "Man of the Millennium." The vote wasn't close. Two-thirds of them chose Genghis Khan.

Other Important Empires

Throughout history, powerful individuals and nations have gone beyond their original boundaries to assemble far-reaching empires. These are the largest.

In the late nineteenth and early twentieth centuries, people said, "The sun never sets on the *British Empire*." That was because its lands stretched around the entire globe. With more than 14 million square miles, it was the largest empire in world history. It included Australia, Canada, India, and large parts of Africa.

The second largest, at just under 14 million square miles, was the *Communist Empire*. Most of it consisted of the Union of Soviet Socialist Republics (USSR), or Soviet Union. The USSR was formed in 1922, five years after the Communist Party took over the government of Russia. It consisted of Russia and fourteen other countries. Shortly after the end of World War II in 1945, the Soviets installed communist governments in several eastern European nations. At about the same time, communists seized control of China and some smaller Asian countries. At first, the Soviet Union and China were close allies. But they had serious disagreements in the early 1960s, weakening the international communist movement. In 1991, the Soviet Union collapsed, though China remains under communist rule.

The *Spanish Empire*, which reached its peak in the latter part of the eighteenth century, began with Columbus's discovery of the New World in 1492. It contained about 7.5 million square miles, with huge swaths of land in Europe and in South, Central, and North America.

Within a century of the death of Muhammad, the founder of Islam, in 632, his successors, the caliphs, had conquered more than 5 million square miles. Most of these lands were in southwest Asia, central Asia, and North Africa. Known as the *Caliphate*, this empire endured until about 945.

The *French Colonial Empire* in the nineteenth and early twentieth centuries encompassed nearly 5 million square miles. Most of the territory was in Africa and parts of Southeast Asia.

During World War II, the *Japanese Empire* covered nearly 3 million square miles, though much of that was empty ocean. At the same time, the *German Third Reich* (*Reich* means "empire") under Adolf Hitler consisted of almost 1.5 million square miles.

In ancient times, the *Roman Empire* and the *Persian Empire*, at a little over 2 million square miles apiece, were each about the same size as Alexander's empire.

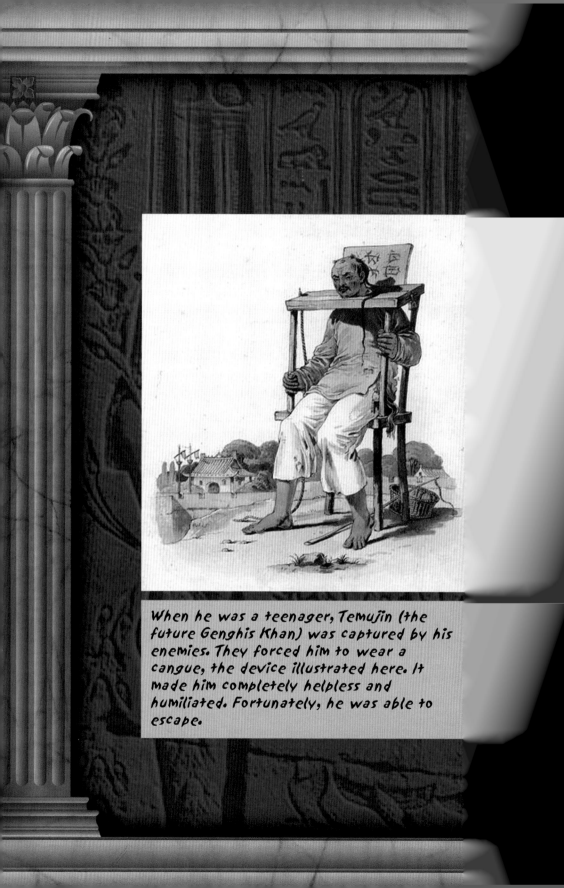

When he was a teenager, Temujin (the future Genghis Khan) was captured by his enemies. They forced him to wear a cangue, the device illustrated here. It made him completely helpless and humiliated. Fortunately, he was able to escape.

CHAPTER
TWO

STRUGGLE FOR SURVIVAL

No one is sure when the boy who would become Genghis Khan was born. At least one Muslim scholar has claimed it was in 1155. Others maintain that it was in 1167. The most commonly accepted year, 1162, is the date recognized in present-day Mongolia.

The boy's father, Yesugei, was a leader of the Borijins, one of several clans of the Mongol tribe. The Mongols, in turn, were one of more than half a dozen nomadic tribes living in central Asia. One day Yesugei was hunting when he saw a young man from the Merkid tribe traveling with his beautiful new bride, Hoelun. Yesugei rode home and summoned his two brothers. The three of them took off in pursuit of the couple. Hoelun knew her new husband would die if he tried to fight. She urged him to ride away. Yesugei and his brothers chased him, but he escaped. When they returned, Hoelun cried bitterly at her loss. Yesugei didn't care. He took her home to become his second wife. This was hardly unusual. Among these tribes, kidnapping was one of the most common ways of acquiring a wife.

About a year later, Hoelun gave birth to a son. According to the clan's custom, infants were named for important recent events. Not long before, Yesugei had killed a man named Temujin, a member of the Tartar tribe. He gave that name to his new boy. Writing many years later, the anonymous author of *The Secret History of the Mongols*—one of the few sources of information about this era—wrote that the infant was born clutching a blood clot. That was considered a significant omen of future greatness.

Yesugei and Hoelun had four more children, who were born at two-year intervals: three sons—Khasar, Kachun, and Temuge—and a daughter, Temulun. Yesugei had another wife, Sochigel, with whom he had two sons: Begter, who was born before Temujin, and Belgutei.

All these children were born into a harsh land. There was no time to coddle or spoil them. Almost as soon as they could walk, they were given important chores. They watched over their precious horses and cattle, learned to recognize and pick edible plants, churned milk, and did other tasks.

Of much more importance, they learned how to ride horses, perhaps even before they could walk. When they grew a little older, they would also learn how to shoot a bow and arrow from a galloping horse—often turning completely around in the saddle and firing with deadly accuracy. They became virtually an extension of their horses, giving them an unprecedented amount of mobility.

"When a Mongol is separated from his horse, what is there left for him to do but die,"[1] ran a tribal proverb. Yet to modern eyes, accustomed to watching graceful thoroughbred horses pounding along racetracks in famous events such as the Kentucky Derby, the horses that Temujin learned to ride would not have seemed very impressive. Mongol horses were small, scarcely larger than ponies, with thick necks and oddly shaped heads. While they didn't look pretty by modern standards, they were exceptionally hardy. They had to be in order to survive bleak conditions that would kill nearly any other type of horse. They endured the cold subarctic blasts that swept across the steppes, and they somehow managed to find food even in the arid winters. Their stamina was legendary. They were capable of feats of endurance that would be fatal to almost any other type of horse.

When Temujin was nine, Yesugei took him to another tribe, the Onggirat. There the boy was betrothed to a ten-year-old girl, Bortei. According to custom, Temujin stayed with his future bride's family. Yesugei headed home. On the way, he met a band of Tartars, against whom he had led several raids. Very unwisely, he decided to accept their offer of hospitality, apparently believing that he could keep his identity secret from them. He was wrong. Someone recognized him. But no one raised a hand against him. Instead, they invited him to join them for a meal.

Soon Yesugei rode away, but shortly he started feeling ill. By the time he returned home three days later, he realized what had happened. The Tartars had slipped a slow-acting but very powerful poison into his food. Yesugei remained alive long enough to identify his killers—a crime for which they would pay very dearly in future years.

His death was a disaster for his family. Temujin was summoned home. The members of his clan refused to allow a nine-year-old boy to become their leader. Instead, they moved away and abandoned the family, expecting them to die. Hoelun had other ideas. Grimly, she struggled for survival, desperately seeking out food to feed her family. She dug up edible roots and picked berries. She harvested wild garlic and onions. The boys helped out, catching a few fish in the river and small animals such as marmots and mice. The family was usually hungry, but they were alive.

Nor were they entirely alone. When he was eleven, Temujin made a friend named Jamuka from another family that often camped nearby. The two boys were distantly related and wanted to become closer. They became *anda*, which roughly means "blood brothers." They mixed a few drops of their blood in a cup of milk, and each took a drink.

Temujin also made enemies: his two half-brothers, who took away a fish that he and his brother Khasar had caught. Surprisingly, Hoelun urged him to accept the slight. She explained that their only hope of survival was to stick together. Temujin didn't listen to her. He and Khasar crept up on Begter, who was watching their horses. Drawing their bows, they shot him.

Food probably wasn't the only reason for this feud. With both boys now in their early teens and not far apart in age, they would have been competing to become head of the family. By killing Begter, Temujin had eliminated his rival—but he had exchanged one problem for a much larger one.

Hoelun's worries were well founded. Her family had been outcasts for several years. Now they were outlaws. The crime caused the Tayichiuds, another Mongol clan, to come after the family. They not only wanted to punish Temujin for his action but also to remove him as a potential rival for leadership. The desperate family tried to hide themselves in a nearby forest. The clan leaders shouted, "Send out your older brother Temujin. We have no need for the rest of you."[2]

Temujin hopped onto a horse and rode away, fleeing into the deepest part of the forest. He was soon captured. For some reason, the Tayichiuds chose not to kill Temujin—at least not right away. Rather, they decided to make his life miserable. They forced him to wear a *cangue*, a heavy wooden yoke that encircled his neck and wrists. Its weight and shape made him uncomfortable whether he tried to rest or walk around. He was virtually helpless, unable even to feed himself.

Wearing the *cangue* in humiliation, Temujin was passed among different families. One evening, he had a chance to escape. He was left with a single guard while the rest of the clan was celebrating. He swung the *cangue*, knocking out his guard. He knew he had no chance of outrunning his captors. He plunged into a river, allowing only his face to show. The furious Tayichiuds began searching for him. For several hours he eluded capture. Then he was spotted. But the man who saw him wasn't a clan member. He took pity on Temujin and didn't reveal his presence.

The man and his family did even more. When the pursuers moved farther away, they cut off the *cangue* and burned it. Then they hid Temujin in a wagon full of wool. The ruse was nearly discovered, but the man told the clan members that anyone who tried to hide there would suffocate in the fierce summer heat. Then he gave Temujin an old horse, some food, and water. The boy galloped away and managed to track down his family.

Their troubles weren't over. A group of raiders took away all but one of the family's horses. Among people who depended so completely on those animals, it was a potential disaster. Temujin took the final horse and set off by himself in pursuit. With the aid of Boorchu, a boy he met along the way, he managed to reclaim the stolen horses. The family's fortunes seemed to improve from this point as they began a cattle herd and added some other animals.

Now it was time to think of marriage. Temujin, who was probably sixteen at this time, reclaimed Bortei. Her father had remained faithful to the word he had given to Yesugei. Bortei came to Temujin with a dowry of some animals, a few servants, and a coat of sable.

Marrying Bortei was one of the best decisions Temujin ever made. She had an exceptionally strong character. When he was faced with making important decisions, he often asked her advice.

The next step was to begin claiming the leadership of his clan. Temujin knew he would need assistance from a more powerful leader to achieve this end. He decided to approach Toghril, the leader of the Kereyid tribe. Toghril and Yesugei had been *anda*. To sweeten the deal, Temujin offered Toghril the sable coat that Bortei had given him. Toghril accepted the alliance. By the time Temujin returned home, he had attracted the loyalty of a young man named Jelme, who along with Boorchu would eventually prove to be one of Temujin's best commanders.

Not long afterward, a band of several hundred Merkids attacked his camp. They were seeking revenge for Yesugei's abduction of

Hoelun many years earlier. Temujin, his brothers, his mother, Boorchu, and Jelme fled up the mountain Burkhan Khaldun. Bortei, who did not have a horse, was captured. One of the Merkids jubilantly took her as his wife. Temujin remained on the mountain for several days. When he emerged, he said that the mountain had saved his life, and he vowed to pray to it every day.

The loss of Bortei presented him with a fateful choice. He didn't have enough men to challenge the Merkids. With kidnapping a common method of acquiring wives, no one would have thought less of him for accepting the loss of Bortei, then replacing her in the same way. But he realized that even if he kidnapped a new bride, he would always be at the mercy of other raiders. There was only one thing to do. He had to become involved in the seemingly ceaseless rounds of clan and tribal warfare on the steppes and make himself powerful enough to keep potential raiders away from him.

There was another reason for not giving up Bortei. Temujin appears to have genuinely and deeply loved her. He appealed to Toghril for help. Toghril agreed. He had issues with the Merkids himself.

He told Temujin to seek the aid of another rising young leader: Jamuka, Temujin's *anda*. Though Temujin was no stranger to fighting, this was the first time that he would be involved in an actual battle. With his two allies, he easily overcame the Merkids and was reunited with his wife. Some months later she gave birth to a son, Jochi. It wasn't clear whether the Merkid or Temujin was the boy's father. It didn't appear to matter, as Temujin raised Jochi as his own son.

As he ended his teenage years, Temujin had survived several serious tests. He had made some friends and some enemies. For the former, rewards lay in store. For the latter, payback. Very serious payback.

Mongol Religion

It was in keeping with Mongol tradition for Temujin not only to pray on the mountain of Burkhan Khaldun, but also to pray *to* the mountain, to the spirit that he believed resided there. The religion in which he had been raised was a type of nature worship known as animism. Animism emphasizes the importance of the spirit world.

The Mongols believed that powerful spirits lived everywhere, from the dancing flames of the fires that warmed them at night, to the winds that howled across the steppes. These spirits were always to be treated with the utmost respect. Mongols risked severe beatings or even outright death from their fellows if they did anything to offend these spirits. Some of these "crimes" seem obvious, such as urinating in a stream. But something seemingly as innocent as putting a knife into a fire or washing out cooking pots, under certain circumstances, could invite punishment.

Tengri

Above all, there was the sky. Because Mongolia is hundreds of miles inland from major bodies of water, there is very little humidity and therefore few clouds. The Mongols lived their lives in almost constant sunshine and sparkling blue skies. The huge expanse of sky was Tengri, the supreme Mongol god.

Animism wasn't the only religion in the steppes. Many people in the area believed in other religions, primarily Buddhism, Christianity, and Islam. After Temujin secured supreme power for himself and took the name of Genghis Khan, he did something revolutionary. He allowed complete freedom of religion. Many historians believe that he was the first significant ruler in world history to take this step. There was a practical reason for his decision. He knew that it could be destructive to try to force his people to accept a single religion. Taking a further step, he exempted the leaders of every religion from military service and from taxation.

Genghis Khan and the other Mongols lived in
these structures, which are called gers. They
were very portable and easy to take down and
set up again at a new location. Many people in
Mongolia still live in gers.

CHAPTER
THREE

THE NAME THAT WOULD MAKE HISTORY

For nearly two years after regaining Bortei, Temujin and Jamuka stayed together. However, it soon became apparent that both young men were ambitious, both were gifted military leaders, and both inspired loyalty from their followers. There was an additional complication. Even though they were related, Jamuka claimed that his lineage put him on a higher level than Temujin.

The two young men parted company abruptly. One day Jamuka wanted to call a halt to the day's progress. Bortei urged her husband to keep going. A few words from her were enough to undo the friendship. Some of Jamuka's men went with Temujin. The incident marked the beginning of Temujin's rise as a leader. It also marked the beginning of a long-running feud between Temujin and Jamuka. Both sought to enlist families and clans, hoping to become a khan, someone who could pull all the Mongols together.

Eight years later, Temujin believed that he was ready. He invoked a traditional assembly called a *khuriltai* and declared himself as the khan even though Jamuka still had more supporters. He instituted a new tradition among the Mongols, by rewarding people on the basis of merit rather than family association. Thus his first two followers—Boorchu and Jelme—had more authority than his brothers.

Temujin was careful to assure the still-powerful Toghril that he wasn't trying to challenge his authority. He explained that his only goal was to unite the scattered Mongols. Toghril and the Kereyids would still be the leaders.

A year later, the simmering hostility between Temujin and Jamuka came to a boil—literally. One of Temujin's men killed a kinsman of Jamuka's. The enraged Jamuka launched a raid on Temujin's camp. Temujin and most of his men managed to escape. About seventy didn't. They were bound and thrown into kettles filled with scalding water. The atrocity backfired. Even for people used to killing, the tactic seemed unduly cruel. In a sense, Temujin lost the battle but won the war. More and more people left Jamuka and joined Temujin.

In 1196, there was another turning point. The Chin, rulers of one of the regions into which China was divided, had always tried to pit the nomad tribes against each other. That way the tribes could never unite and threaten Chin rule. They persuaded Toghril to attack the Tartars. Toghril asked Temujin to join him. It must have been an easy sell. Temujin had never forgotten that the Tartars had murdered his father.

The campaign went well. For Temujin, it had two results. He was very impressed with the goods that he captured, since the Tartars' land lay close to the major trade routes. He also realized that this method of warfare would never end. Tribes that were allied one year could be enemies the next.

The following year, he attacked a nearby tribe, the Jurkins. They hadn't joined him as originally promised when he attacked the Tartars. Even worse, they had raided his camp while he was away fighting. Temujin defeated them easily. Normally in nomad warfare, a few members of a vanquished tribe would be taken prisoner and the rest released. That allowed them to reorganize and forge fresh alliances with other tribes—perpetuating the endless cycle of war. Temujin

This illustration shows a Tartar warrior. The bow he holds may seem very small to us. Yet it was a very effective weapon. Even riding full speed on horseback, men who were trained in its use could hit targets hundreds of feet away.

decided on a new approach. He executed the aristocratic leaders. Then he occupied Jurkin lands and distributed the tribe's members among his followers—not as slaves but as fellow Mongols. He even had his mother adopt a Jurkin boy—in effect, giving the child status as his own brother.

Four years of relative peace followed. Then in 1201, Jamuka made his move. He summoned his own *khuriltai* and had himself declared gur-khan, which means "khan of all khans." He also challenged Toghril. Temujin and Toghril won the first battle, but Jamuka escaped with many of his men.

In 1202, Temujin went after the Tartars again. He was victorious and decided to incorporate them as he had done with the Jurkins. Again he gave a Tartar boy to his mother. He also took two Tartar women as his wives. Because the Tartars were much better known than the Mongols, the name *Tartar* eventually became at least synonymous with, if not more famous than, *Mongol*. Temujin used a different term: He increasingly began calling his followers "the People of the Felt Walls." Felt was the material they used as the outer covering of their *gers*, the mobile homes in which they lived.

This conquest only heightened the tension between Temujin and Jamuka. It also made Toghril more apprehensive. In 1203, Temujin proposed a marriage between his son Jochi and one of Toghril's daughters. Toghril refused. Then he had an idea. He sent word that he had changed his mind. He would be happy to unite the two families.

Temujin set off with a small band. With Toghril likely to die soon, the marriage would unite the Kereyids and the Mongols. This new grouping would become one of the most powerful on the steppes. When Temujin was just a few miles away, he learned that Toghril's offer was bogus. Toghril was planning to kill him and everyone with him. Temujin fled.

Once again Temujin faced a crisis. Now that he was a fugitive, could he keep the loyalty of his followers? He needn't have worried. He sent word of the betrayal to them, and they responded by flocking to his banner. With Temujin at their head, they attacked Toghril, who was celebrating because he had apparently eliminated Temujin as a threat. Toghril and Jamuka fled to the Naimans, the final remaining tribe that Temujin hadn't conquered.

In 1204, Temujin took on the Naimans and defeated them. They had already executed Toghril, but Jamuka escaped with a handful of men. Several months later these men betrayed Jamuka, allowing Temujin to take him prisoner. Temujin offered Jamuka a place in his army.

"Now that the world is ready for you, what use is there in my becoming your companion?" Jamuka replied. "On the contrary, sworn brother, in the black night I would haunt your dreams, in the bright day I would trouble your thoughts. I would be the louse in your collar, the splinter in your door-panel. . . . Now put a quick end to me."[1]

Temujin had no choice. He had to execute his *anda*. Jamuka had one final request: that none of his blood be shed. Temujin granted him this favor. He ordered his men to pile heavy rocks on Jamuka's chest. His friend was crushed to death.

The steppes of central Asia are somewhat similar to the Great Plains area in the United States. They consist of gently rolling hills, many of which are covered with grass for grazing. As you can see, there are very few trees.

After Jamuka, there were no more challenges to Temujin's rule. He called another *khuriltai*. This time he chose a new title for himself: Chinggis Khan, meaning "universal" or "oceanic" ruler. Later the name would be written as *Genghis*, the spelling by which future generations would come to know him.

Temujin, now Genghis Khan, had united all the tribes of the steppes; they became known collectively as Mongols. He appeared to be at the high point of his career. Yet he was just getting started.

Genghis realized that his tenure at the top could be quite limited. Bitter experience had taught him the sometimes shifting nature of allegiances. One primary method of reducing the risk was to mix up the members of different tribes in the army. No man could transfer from one unit to another without express permission. The goal was to make every man completely loyal to the army. The army, in turn, would owe its loyalty to Genghis. To discourage attempts on his life, he formed a *keshig*, or personal bodyguard. Originally less than a hundred men, it grew to include thousands of troops.

At the same time, he began formulating a code of laws, which became known as the *Yasa*. Eventually it encompassed nearly every aspect of military and civilian life, and became one of the main reasons for the success of his empire.

Now that he had an army, he had to do something with it. It had to have a purpose. At first his forays consisted of raids against the most logical target: the Chinese kingdom of the Tanguts. The Tanguts could put up little resistance, and in 1209 they agreed to a peace treaty that recognized the superiority of Genghis Khan. The victory gave him access to the Silk Road, lucrative trade routes that stretched between China and Persia (present-day Iran).

The next objective was the much larger and more powerful Chin Empire, which encompassed much of northern China. Between 1209 and 1211, the Mongols made some modest territorial gains. The battles heated up in 1211 when Genghis invaded the Chin Empire with his entire army. It was a risk. His men were outnumbered by about three or four to one. It didn't matter. The Mongols' superior mobility allowed them to outmaneuver the Chin armies. The Mongols also adopted a cruel but effective strategy. They stayed away from cities and devastated the countryside. They burned farmhouses, took some of the crops for their own and destroyed the rest, then ruined the fields. They even choked irrigation ditches so that land under cultivation would dry up and become useless for growing further crops.

Part of the reason for this destruction was cultural. As men who had always lived in the open and on the move, they had contempt for people who were tied to the land. Another was practical. By destroying farmland and allowing it to revert to pasture, the Mongols assured

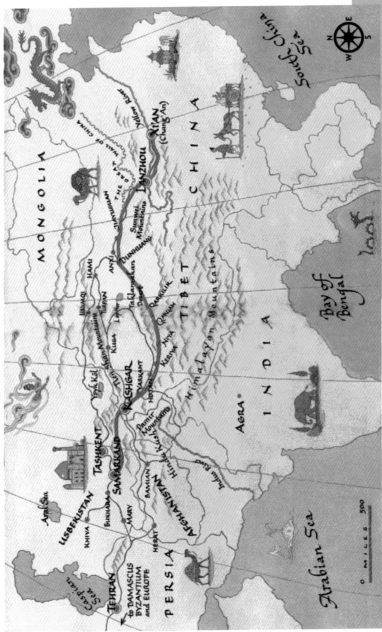

The famous Silk Road flourished for many centuries. Traders and travelers were able to travel in almost complete safety for thousands of miles. The thick red line shows the most heavily traveled section. Checkpoints in circles are the richest towns along the way. Lighter red lines show additional routes.

themselves of plenty of grazing land for their horses as they went back and forth between China and their homeland.

After three years of fighting, the Mongols had surrounded Zhongdu, the Chin capital, but they couldn't penetrate the city's defensive walls. The Chin made a deal. They gave the Mongols huge amounts of gold, silver, silk, stallions, and other treasures. They also gave Genghis a princess as one of his wives. Genghis returned home that fall, feeling that he had achieved a victory—the Chin had apparently accepted him as the region's primary ruler. The Chin, however, also felt good. They had managed to buy off the invaders.

The next year, the Chin leaders abandoned the city and moved farther south, seeking to get as far away from the Mongols as possible. Genghis believed that the Chin had broken their agreement. When the Mongols returned to Zhongdu in the spring of 1215, the attitude was different. The inhabitants felt abandoned. They opened the city's gates. The Mongols poured inside. The city was looted of all its valuables, and huge portions of it were torched. Thousands of people were cut down.

For the first time, the Mongols had to assume responsibility for governing a land they had conquered. One result of the Chinese campaigns was a string of caravans loaded with trade goods. Genghis Khan found himself in the import-export business. His attention turned from war to warehouses. He had to find space to store all his accumulated goods.

Thousands of miles away, a seemingly trivial incident would soon turn Genghis Khan's attention back to war. It would result in the deaths of uncounted numbers of people.

The Mongols' Mobile Homes

FYI
For Your Info

When Genghis Khan referred to himself as the leader of "the People of the Felt Walls," he was literally correct. Because the Mongols were nomads, people who wandered across the steppes, they had no fixed homes. Rather, they took their homes with them, loading them onto carts that were drawn by oxen or other animals. They would move several times a year, each time settling in an area that had abundant pastures for grazing their livestock.

These homes, called gers, were similar to large tents. Circular, between 15 and 30 feet in diameter and weighing several hundred pounds, they had two main parts: a framework made of light wooden sticks, and several layers of felt, made from sheep's wool, that covered the framework.

It took a family only an hour or two to set up their ger. The first step was to erect the circular framework. It consisted of several sections of flat sticks arranged in a crisscrossing pattern, similar to a net. These would be lashed together with strips of rawhide. There was space for a door, which faced south—both for good luck and to admit sunlight. Longer poles were attached to the top of the wall. They were fastened to a ring of heavy wood in the center that was about ten feet off the ground. Then layers of felt—as many as seven or eight during the winter months—were laid over this framework. Each layer of felt was treated with fat to make it virtually waterproof and windproof. The floor was covered with wooden planks or felt.

With the ger set up, the next step was to bring the family's belongings inside. The hearth was placed in the center, with the overhead ring remaining open to allow smoke to escape. Beds—which were also places to sit—and colorful chests were placed along the walls. The "man of the house" always sat directly opposite the door, with women to the east and men to the west. Horns tied to the walls served as hooks to hang clothing, meat, and weapons.

The ger was ideal for its environment. It was warm in winter and cool in summer. Even today, many people in Mongolia live in gers.

These are modern-day views of Samarkand (top) and Bukhara (bottom). They were among the many cities that Genghis Khan and his army conquered. They were especially wealthy during the Mongol era.

CHAPTER

FOUR

"I AM THE PUNISHMENT OF GOD"

The western part of the Silk Road was controlled by Khwarazm Shah, whose empire had benefited greatly from centuries of trade. Cities such as Samarkand and Bukhara had become fabulously wealthy because of the caravans that stopped there. In 1216 Genghis sent a letter to the shah, boasting of his conquests and referring to the shah as "my most cherished son."[1] He wanted a trade agreement that would allow caravans to pass freely between the two empires.

Two years later, a caravan departing from Mongol territory arrived in the town of Otrar. The governor, suspecting that the caravan's 450 members were Mongol spies, had all of them put to death. Genghis sent three ambassadors to the shah to protest and demand compensation. The shah responded by executing one and burning off the beards of the other two. He knew it meant war. Apparently he felt that his army of 400,000 men could easily deal with the Mongols. He couldn't have been more wrong.

Genghis knew that the upcoming battles would be more difficult than the ones in China because his men would be traveling much farther. In view of his advancing age—by this time he was well into his fifties—and the possibility that he might not return, he also had to designate a successor. The successor would come from among his sons by Bortei, his principal wife. Jochi, the eldest, couldn't be considered because of his doubtful paternity. The second was Chaghadai, a good administrator. For some reason, Genghis didn't think very highly of him. The third son was Ogodei, the smartest of the group and a good general but prone to alcohol. The youngest, Tolui, was even more of a drunkard but a brilliant general. Genghis finally settled on Ogodei but made the other three swear an oath of allegiance.

He divided his army into four groups. The first, under Chaghadai and Ogodei, advanced to Otrar. The governor knew what lay in store for him if he was captured. He settled down, confident that he and his portion of the troops—80,000 men—could withstand a long siege. Two other Mongol forces ranged up and down the shah's dominions. The fourth was under Genghis Khan's direct command. It seemed to vanish from the face of the earth. In reality, Genghis took a route that was thought to be impenetrable and was therefore left unguarded. Without warning, he turned up at the gates of Bukhara. The garrison tried to fight their way to freedom. All were slaughtered. The city's frightened inhabitants quickly opened the gates, hoping that Genghis would spare their lives. He did. Then he rode into the largest mosque and summoned the citizens. "I am the punishment of God," he told them. "If you had not committed great sins, he would not have sent a punishment like me."[2] After looting the city, destroying many of its buildings and killing some of the people, he allowed the survivors to flee. They scattered throughout the shah's kingdom, bearing news in graphic detail of what had happened. Genghis hoped that their accounts would frighten and demoralize everyone who heard them.

The strategy bore fruit. Samarkand had been expected to hold out for a year. It fell within five days.

Then it was Otrar's turn. The garrison and most of the town's inhabitants were slaughtered. Genghis ordered the governor, Inalchuq, to be taken alive. He was taken to Samarkand, where Genghis executed him by pouring molten silver into his eyes and ears.

In the meantime, the shah had escaped. Genghis detailed part of his army to pursue him. The chase led to the shores of the Caspian Sea. There the shah ripped off his elegant clothing, put on rags, and narrowly escaped his pursuers to a small island, where he died in misery.

The ease with which he captured Samarkand was very revealing to Genghis Khan. It demonstrated that the shah's command of his territories had not been very strong. These territories not only yielded up great amounts of captured trade goods, but also provided more land for the growing Mongol empire.

Some captured cities escaped with a minimum of looting. Others lost nearly all their possessions, though the inhabitants were allowed to remain. If a city resisted the Mongols' demand to surrender, it could expect heavy loss of life. The worst fate was reserved for cities that surrendered, then tried to rebel when the army moved on. The citizens of Nishapur, for example, initially supplied Mongol troops as they passed through and were left in peace. But when the Mongols reappeared, they tried to fight back. One of the Mongol casualties was Tokuchar, a member of Genghis's family.

Tokuchar's death sealed the fate of Nishapur. When the Mongols captured the city, they slaughtered every person there. They cut off the heads of all their victims and placed them in neat rows according to age and gender.

The Mongol army spent several years roaming through the shah's kingdom, capturing dozens of cities and sending vast amounts of plunder back to Mongolia. They also captured thousands of craftsmen and other people with unique skills, and these prisoners accompanied the plunder.

Subodei, one of Genghis's generals, led a detachment in what historians regard as one of the most remarkable feats in the history of mounted warfare. He traveled thousands of miles through what is

This contemporary re-creation shows the Mongol army on the attack. While it may appear disorganized, Genghis Khan instilled a very high level of discipline and mobility among his men. These qualities enabled the Mongols to repeatedly defeat enemies with much larger armies.

today Azerbaijan and Georgia, then up the western shore of the Caspian Sea into Russia, where, even though he was outnumbered, he won several notable victories.

Genghis himself had other things on his mind. He had found a Chinese philosopher, with whom he had numerous conversations about death. He started for home in 1223 and arrived two years later. There was much to take care of. Much of the Chin territory had been lost. And he had one final score to settle.

The Mongol Army

With a very few exceptions, as soon as a Mongol boy turned fourteen he was considered eligible for military service, and he was expected to report for duty with four or five horses. He would be assigned to the basic unit of the army: the *arban*, a group of ten men. Ten *arbans* formed a *jagun*. A *minghan*, or regiment, consisted of ten *jaguns*. The largest unit was a division, or *tumen*, with ten *minghans*—a total of 10,000 men. The men practiced together, perfecting numerous battlefield tactics. Together with their discipline and the mobility that they gained from their horses, these tactics helped them defeat enemies that had many more men.

Each Mongol warrior wore a silk undershirt. While that may sound luxurious, there was a practical reason. Silk consists of very densely woven threads. An arrow would drive the silk into the wound around the arrowhead, forming a kind of cocoon that was much easier—and far less painful—to extract than if the arrow had been driven into bare flesh.

All the men were armed with two bows and several dozen arrows, which they shot with devastating accuracy from distances of up to two football fields laid end to end. Some also carried small swords and javelins, while the more heavily armed had lances, heavy swords, and battle-axes. In addition to their weapons, the men packed cooking utensils, spare clothing, water bottles, and other gear in saddlebags made from cow stomachs. These saddlebags could be inflated and were useful as flotation devices when the army crossed rivers.

Genghis combined the men's love of hunting with military drills. During the winter months, when there was no fighting, the men would engage in mass hunts with other members of their units. They would drive their quarry in front of them before encircling it and killing it.

Part of their success came from developing an elaborate and effective signal system. They used flags, torches, and long-distance riders who carried messages. The units not only stayed in constant communication but also remained under the control of their commanding officer.

In short, the Mongols composed a professional standing army—virtually unprecedented for that era.

Khublai Khan was Genghis Khan's grandson. He became known as the Great Khan because he was able to conquer all of China, something his grandfather was never able to accomplish. His court was famous for its high level of learning and lavish entertainments.

CHAPTER
FIVE

THE EMPEROR DIES, THE EMPIRE LIVES ON

When he had set out for the shah's territory seven years earlier, Genghis had asked the Tanguts for soldiers. They had refused with an insult: "If Genghis Khan was not strong enough to undertake the struggle against Khwarazm, he should not aspire to the role of emperor."[1] When Genghis received the reply, he was too busy to deal with the situation. But he hadn't forgotten. Now it was time to take revenge on the Tanguts. In 1226, Genghis set out at the head of his army. Within a year the campaign was nearly over.

The same was true of Genghis's life. In August 1227, he died. No one knows the reason. Some sources say he fell from a horse and sustained severe injuries. Others say he was wounded by an arrow. Or he may have simply died from natural causes. Living into one's sixties was rare in that era. At his orders, the news was kept secret from the army until they captured the Tangut capital. When the soldiers learned of his death, they became so enraged that they killed nearly everyone living in the city.

In the meantime, a picked force of men conveyed their leader's body to its final resting place on Burkhan Khaldun. To keep the exact location a secret, anything living that the men encountered en route—

animals and humans alike—was put to the sword. To this day, no one knows the site of the tomb.

The death of its founder didn't slow down the Mongol war machine. Under the leadership of Ogodei, in the next four years the Mongols acquired more territory in northern China, conquered Korea, and extended their campaigns in the west. An army commanded by Batu, one of Genghis's grandsons, crossed the steppes of Russia. The Mongols sacked Moscow and Kiev, then turned south. By 1241 they were in Hungary. They brushed aside and nearly annihilated European armies that greatly outnumbered them. There seemed to be no reason why they couldn't keep going, all the way to the Atlantic Ocean.

"In packed churches across northern Europe sermons were being conducted before a terrified population, while prayers were offered up pleading: '. . . from the fury of the Tartars [the Europeans' name for the Mongols], oh Lord deliver us,' "[2] reports historian Robert Marshall.

Perhaps their prayers were answered. Ogodei died late that year. All the Mongol chiefs were summoned back for a *khuriltai* to select his replacement. As mysteriously as they had appeared—Europe had little comprehension of the Mongols' distant homeland—they disappeared. Though they controlled Russia for many years, never again would they threaten the rest of Europe.

The same did not hold true for much of Asia. With Mongke— another of Genghis's grandsons—becoming the Great Khan in 1251, Mongol armies ravaged Persia and nearly all of China. The region was spared further suffering when Mongke died in 1259. The empire began to split up, as four other grandsons each held significant khanates. The most famous of these was Khublai Khan. Even though he was eventually designated as the Great Khan, he never had the same power or prestige as his grandfather. One reason was that Khublai wanted to abandon the nomadic ways of his ancestors. He was heavily influenced by Chinese teachers as he grew up, and eventually came to feel more at home among the Chinese than he did among the Mongols. He built sumptuous summer and winter palaces in China.

In 1279 Khublai Khan completed the conquest of China that his grandfather had begun some seventy years earlier. By then, he had also welcomed a guest from Italy who had traveled thousands of miles to meet him. It was Marco Polo. Two decades later, Polo wrote a book called *A Description of the World* about his experiences. It made "Marco Polo" a household name in much of Europe.

More than six centuries later, the communist rulers of Mongolia would try to remove Genghis Khan's name as a household word. By then, his empire was only a distant memory. It had begun to break up during the 14th and 15th centuries, though a descendent—Sayid Alim Khan—ruled Bukhara until a communist takeover in 1920. Soon after Sayid Alim's overthrow, Genghis's homeland in Mongolia fell under the rule of the Soviet Union. The Soviets tracked down his other descendents and shot them. They referred to him as "the bloodthirsty barbarian Genghis Khan."[3] But Mongolians continued to revere him. With the breakup of the Soviet Union in 1991, it soon became permissible for Mongolian citizens to publicly exhibit remembrances of Genghis Khan, such as postage stamps, posters, and banners.

In the rest of the world, his reputation remains mixed. To some, he is the "bloodthirsty barbarian" to whom the communists referred. No one will ever know how many people met their death at the hands of Genghis Khan's fearsome fighters. Entire populations were uprooted from their homes and forced to live elsewhere.

To others, he helped to shape the modern world. His tolerance of religions such as Buddhism, Christianity, and Islam influenced the way in which those beliefs grew and spread. His conquests changed political boundaries. He helped to develop what today we call the "global village," in which ideas and goods flow freely among different cultures.

Marco Polo was a Venetian merchant who spent many years with Khublai Khan. He became one of Khublai's most trusted advisers. Polo traveled to many remote parts of Khublai's empire. He brought back accounts of all he had seen. When he wrote down these accounts and published them in Europe, many people thought he was lying.

But there can be no doubt that the little boy who nearly perished when he and his family were abandoned by their kinsmen on the harsh steppes of central Asia grew up to make an indelible mark on the history of the world.

THE MONGOL KHANS DYNASTY

Genghis (Chinggis) Kahn (d. 1227)
Jochi (d. 1227)
Ogodei (r. 1229–41)
Chaghadai (d. 1242)
Tolui (d. 1233)
Guyug (r. 1246–48)
Batu (d. 1255)
Berke
Mongke (r. 1251–59)
Khublai (r. 1260–94)
Hulegu (d. 1265)
Arigh Boke

Genghis Khan's family tree. The row just above Genghis shows his four sons. The others are his grandsons. The letter "d" in the list in the lower left means the year the particular person died. The letter "r" stands for "reigned" and indicates the years in which he ruled.

FYI
For Your Info

Marco Polo presents a letter to Khublai Khan

Much of what we know about living conditions in the Mongol Empire comes from Marco Polo. Marco was born in Venice, Italy, in 1254, shortly after his father and uncle began a trip that ended in Khublai Khan's court. The two men came back in 1269, then—accompanied by Marco—set out again two years later for a return visit. Marco was very impressed by what he saw when he met Khublai Khan.

The favorable impression was mutual. Khublai Khan realized that Marco was a very bright young man. He soon found something for his guest to do. Administrators in his far-flung realm would send Khublai Khan regular reports, but these reports were very limited. They told him nothing of what the different regions were actually like: the people, their living conditions, the types of plants and animals there. Khublai asked Marco to travel throughout the kingdom, then come back and discuss what he saw with him. Khublai wasn't disappointed. Every time Marco returned, he spent hours telling Khublai about everything he had witnessed.

As the years passed, Marco, his father, and his uncle wanted to return home. They were also concerned about Khubilai's advancing age. A new ruler might not treat them as well. But Khublai refused to let them go. He enjoyed their company and they were useful to him. Finally they had their chance to leave. Khublai asked them to escort a Mongol princess to Persia. When they arrived after a long sea voyage, they learned that Khublai had died. They continued to Venice, arriving there in 1295. Hardly anyone recognized them at first.

Soon afterward, Marco was captured by the people of Genoa, a rival Italian city. In prison, he met a writer named Rustichello, who persuaded him to publish an account of his travels. Entitled *A Description of the World*, the book came out in 1299 and was a huge bestseller. However, most people believed that Marco had made up the story. When he was on his deathbed nearly twenty-five years later, a priest wanted him to finally confess that it was all fiction. Marco refused. Everything he wrote was the truth, he said.

Chronology

1162	Temujin is born
1171	Father dies after being poisoned by a band of Tartars
1173	Becomes *anda* with Jamuka
1178	Marries Borte
1179	Birth of first son, Jochi
1181	Separates from Jamuka
1185	Third son, Ogodei, is born (Chaghatai is second son; birth year unknown)
1189	Is named khan
1196	Attacks the Tartars
1197	Overcomes the Jurkins
1202	Defeats Tartars and integrates them into the Mongol tribe
1203	Nearly killed by Toghril and is forced to flee
1204	Defeats Naiman tribe
1205	Kills Jamuka
1206	Takes on name of Genghis Khan and becomes "Universal Ruler" of all Mongols
1209	Accepts submission of the Tanguts
1211	Invades northern China
1215	Storms Chinese city of Zhongdu
1218	Vows revenge when governor of Otrar kills members of a Mongol caravan
1219	Captures Bukhara
1220	Captures Samarkand
1225	Returns to Mongolia
1226	Attacks Tanguts
1227	Dies in August and is buried in an unknown location

Timeline in History

1099	Christian knights capture Jerusalem during the First Crusade.
1131	Persian poet Omar Khayyam dies.
1154	Pope Adrian IV becomes the only English pope.
1187	Muslim leader Saladin recaptures Jerusalem from the Crusaders.
1215	Khublai Khan is born.
1229	Genghis Khan's son Ogodei is selected as Great Khan.
1240	Mongols capture the Ukrainian city of Kiev and virtually destroy it.
1241	Ogodei dies.
1251	Mongke (Khublai's brother) becomes khan.
1254	Marco Polo is born in Venice, Italy.
1260	A weakened Mongol army is defeated by an Egyptian army in present-day Palestine.
1260	Khublai Khan becomes Great Khan.
1271	Marco Polo begins his journey to China; he arrives four years later.
1279	Khublai Khan completes the conquest of China and establishes the Yuan Dynasty.
1281	Khublai Khan sends a force to try to conquer Japan, but it is swept away by a storm that the Japanese call "divine wind," or *kamikaze*.
1294	Khublai Khan dies.
1295	Marco Polo returns to Venice.
1299	Marco Polo publishes *The Description of the World*, an account of his travels in the Mongol Empire; many if not most readers believe that it is fiction.
1324	Marco Polo dies.
1368	The Mongol Yuan Dynasty in China is overthrown.
1400	English poet Geoffrey Chaucer publishes the *Canterbury Tales*; "Squire's Tale" is about Genghis Khan.
1502	Final remaining Mongol army in Russia is destroyed.
1924	Influenced by the Soviet Union, Outer Mongolia becomes the Mongolian People's Republic.
1944	Sayid Alim Khan, Genghis Khan's final reigning descendent, dies.
1992	Mongolian People's Republic adopts new constitution and becomes Mongolia.
2004	Team of Japanese and Mongolian archaeologists announce discovery of Genghis Khan's palace.

Chapter Notes

CHAPTER ONE   A MIGHTY EMPIRE
1. Jack Weatherford, *Genghis Khan and the Making of the Modern World* (New York: Crown Publishers, 2004), p. xvii.
2. *The Secret History of the Mongols: The Life and Times of Chinggis Khan*, translated and annotated by Urgunge Onon (Richmond, Surrey, England: Curzon Press, 2001), p. 13.

CHAPTER TWO   STRUGGLE FOR SURVIVAL
1. Michel Hoang, *Genghis Khan, translated by Ingrid Canfield* (New York: New Amsterdam Books, 1990), p. 20.
2. *The Secret History of the Mongols: The Life and Times of Chinggis Khan*, translated and annotated by Urgunge Onon (Richmond, Surrey, England: Curzon Press, 2001), p. 69.

CHAPTER THREE   THE NAME THAT WOULD MAKE HISTORY
1. *The Secret History of the Mongols: The Life and Times of Chinggis Khan*, translated and annotated by Urgunge Onon (Richmond, Surrey, England: Curzon Press, 2001), pp. 188–89.

CHAPTER FOUR   "I AM THE PUNISHMENT OF GOD"
1. Robert Marshall, *Storm from the East: From Genghis Khan to Khublai Khan* (Berkeley, CA: The University of California Press, 1993), p. 50.
2. Ibid., pp. 53–54.

CHAPTER FIVE   THE EMPEROR DIES, THE EMPIRE LIVES ON
1. Leo de Hartog, *Genghis Khan: Conqueror of the World* (London: I.B. Tauris, 1989), p. 133.
2. Robert Marshall, *Storm from the East: From Genghis Khan to Khublai Khan* (Berkeley, CA: The University of California Press, 1993), p. 13.
3. Jack Weatherford, *Genghis Khan and the Making of the Modern World* (New York: Crown Publishers, 2004), p. 264.

Glossary

anthropology   (an-thruh-PAH-luh-jee)—the study of human beings and their ancestors through time.

imperialism   (im-PEER-ee-uh-lih-zem)—the act of extending a nation's power and influence through conquering other nations and imposing their laws and customs on them.

khan   (KAHN)—a ruler or leader of tribes in medieval Asia.

nomads   (NOE-mads)—people without fixed residences who move from place to place, usually within a certain area, to find grazing land for their animals.

sable   (SAY-bull)—an animal similar to a weasel that has valuable black fur.

Silk Road   The main trade route between China and Rome before a sea route to India was found.

steppe   (STEP)—an expansive, usually flat or rolling treeless grassland in Europe or Asia.

BIOGRAPHY FROM

ANCIENT CIVILIZATIONS

LEGENDS, FOLKLORE, AND STORIES OF ANCIENT WORLDS

For Further Reading

For Young Adults

Greenblatt, Miriam. *Genghis Khan and the Mongol Empire.* Tarrytown, NY: Benchmark Books, 2002.

Lange, Brenda. *Ancient World Leaders: Genghis Khan.* Philadelphia: Chelsea House Publishers, 2003.

Taylor, Robert. *Life in Genghis Khan's Mongolia.* San Diego: Lucent Books, 2000.

Works Consulted

De Hartog, Leo. *Genghis Khan: Conqueror of the World.* London: I.B. Tauris, 1989.

Grousset, Rene. *Conqueror of the World.* Translated by Marian McKellar and Denis Sinor. New York: The Orion Press, 1966.

Hoang, Michel. *Genghis Khan.* Translated by Ingrid Canfield. New York: New Amsterdam Books, 1990.

Lister, R. P. *Genghis Khan.* New York: Cooper Square Press, 2000.

Marshall, Robert. *Storm from the East: From Genghis Khan to Khublai Khan.* Berkeley, CA: The University of California Press, 1993.

The Secret History of the Mongols: The Life and Times of Chinggis Khan. Translated and annotated by Urgunge Onon. Richmond, Surrey, England: Curzon Press, 2001.

Severin, Tim. *In Search of Genghis Khan.* New York: Cooper Square Press, 2003.

Time Frame A.D. 1200–1300: The Mongol Conquests. Alexandria, VA: Time-Life Books, 1989.

Weatherford, Jack. *Genghis Khan and the Making of the Modern World.* New York: Crown Publishers, 2004.

On the Internet

Explorations in Empire, "The Mongols"
http://www.accd.edu/sac/history/keller/Mongols/index.html

History of the Mongol Empire, "History Overview"
http://mongolempire.4t.com/h1_overview.htm

Oestmoen, Per Inge, "Mongol History and Chronology from Ancient Times"
http://www.coldsiberia.org/webdoc3.htm

Travel China Guide: "Silk Road Index"
http://www.travelchinaguide.com/silkroad/

To Rule the Earth . . .
http://www.hostkingdom.net/earthrul.html

Waugh, Daniel C., *Pax Mongolica*
http://www.silk-road.com/artl/paxmongolica.shtml

Index

DUE DATE
